Table Of Contents

Chapter 2: Strategies to Eliminate Your Debt and Student Loans 1
Chapter 3: Opening No-Fee, High-Interest Bank Accounts 1
Chapter 4: Automating Your Finances 1
Chapter 5: Avoiding Late Fees 1
Chapter 6: Budgeting Techniques for Enjoyment 1
Chapter 7: Simplifying Investment Strategies 1
Chapter 8: Managing Major Expenses with Ease 1
Chapter 9: Negotiating a Substantial Raise 1
Chapter 10: Building an Emergency Savings Fund 1
Building an Emergency Savings Fund 1
Chapter 11: Lifestyle Adjustments for Debt Reduction 1
Chapter 12: Conclusion: Your Roadmap to Financial Freedom 1
Chapter 1: Introduction to Automating Your Wealth 1

Introduction to Automating Your Wealth

Understanding the Importance of Financial Automation

In today's fast-paced world, managing finances can feel overwhelming, especially for those with low to medium incomes. Financial automation emerges as a beacon of hope, simplifying the complex landscape of budgeting, saving, and investing. By automating various financial processes, individuals can take control of their financial futures with minimal effort. This automation not only alleviates stress but also allows for a more strategic approach to wealth building, enabling anyone to meet their financial goals more effectively.

One of the most significant advantages of financial automation is its ability to facilitate debt repayment strategies. For recent graduates burdened with student loans or anyone struggling with debt, automating payments can be a game changer. Setting up automatic transfers to pay off debts ensures that you never miss a payment, thereby avoiding costly late fees and penalties. Moreover, by automating the payment of your highest-interest debts first, you can accelerate your journey to financial freedom, freeing up funds for saving and investing sooner than you might have thought possible.

Automating your finances also extends to savings and investment strategies. Opening a no-fee, high-interest savings account is a crucial step toward building a safety net. By automating regular transfers into this account, you can effortlessly grow your savings without even thinking about it. The same principle applies to investments. Imagine deploying a simple, hands-off investment strategy that outperforms traditional financial advisors, all while requiring minimal time and effort on your part. This approach not only builds wealth but also instills a sense of confidence in your financial decisions.

For those balancing major life expenses, such as purchasing a home or planning a wedding, financial automation can provide clarity and ease. By creating a budget that allocates funds toward these significant expenditures, and automating those contributions, you can focus on what truly matters—enjoying the experience without the constant worry of financial strain. Using effective scripts to communicate with creditors or negotiate raises can further bolster your financial position, empowering you to take control of your income and expenses.

Ultimately, adopting financial automation is about making life easier and more fulfilling. It allows you to prioritize your financial goals while still enjoying the activities you love. With the right tools and techniques in place, you can achieve a balanced lifestyle that accommodates both enjoyment and financial responsibility. As you embark on this journey, remember that every step toward automation is a step toward greater financial security and peace of mind. Embrace these strategies and watch how automating your finances can transform your life, paving the way for a brighter, more prosperous future.

The Benefits of Streamlining Your Finances

Streamlining your finances can feel like a daunting task, particularly for those living with low to medium incomes. However, the benefits of simplifying your financial life are profound and far-reaching. By adopting a streamlined approach, you can eliminate debt more quickly, save for future goals, and ultimately gain control over your financial destiny. Imagine a life where you wake up each day knowing your money is working as hard as you do, allowing you to focus on what truly matters—your passions, your family, and your future.

One of the most significant advantages of streamlining your finances is the ability to tackle debt with newfound vigor. Strategies like the snowball or avalanche methods enable you to prioritize your debts and pay them off faster than you ever imagined possible. As you eliminate these financial burdens, you'll feel a sense of relief and empowerment. The process becomes less about sacrifice and more about gaining freedom—freedom to invest in experiences, education, or even a home. You'll be surprised at how quickly your financial landscape can change when you adopt a focused and systematic approach to debt repayment.

Opening no-fee, high-interest bank accounts is another critical aspect of financial streamlining. Many people are unaware that their money could be earning more while incurring fewer costs. By researching and selecting the right banking options, you can protect your savings from unnecessary fees that drain your hard-earned money. This small adjustment can lead to substantial growth in your savings, allowing you to build an emergency fund or save for a significant life event without feeling the pinch. When your finances are streamlined, every dollar counts, and you'll find opportunities to make your money work for you rather than against you.

Automating your finances is an essential strategy for busy individuals who may feel overwhelmed by the demands of daily life. By setting up automatic transfers to savings accounts or investments, you ensure that your money goes exactly where you want it without the need for constant oversight. This method not only simplifies your financial management but also helps you avoid late fees and missed payments, which can be significant obstacles to financial stability. When your finances run smoothly in the background, you can focus on enjoying your life and spending time on what you love, rather than stressing over bills and payments.

Finally, streamlining your finances allows you to manage major expenses with ease. Whether it's buying a car, planning a wedding, or raising children, having a clear financial strategy in place will enable you to approach these situations with confidence. With effective budgeting techniques and the right negotiation tactics, you can navigate these significant life events without breaking the bank. By prioritizing your financial well-being, you create a safety net that allows for enjoyment today while preparing for a secure tomorrow. The journey to financial freedom begins with small, manageable steps, and the rewards are more significant than you might imagine.

Setting Your Financial Goals

Setting your financial goals is an empowering first step toward achieving the financial freedom you deserve. For many individuals with low to medium incomes, the idea of setting goals might seem daunting or even unrealistic. However, by taking a moment to reflect on your aspirations, you can transform your financial landscape and pave the way for a brighter future. Begin by envisioning where you want to be in the next few years. Whether it's eliminating debt, saving for a home, or creating a robust emergency fund, having clear goals provides you with direction and motivation to take actionable steps.

To effectively set your financial goals, it's essential to make them specific, measurable, achievable, relevant, and time-bound (**SMART**). Instead of saying, "I want to save money," try stating, "I will save $5,000 for a down payment on a car within the next 18 months." This approach not only clarifies your target but also allows you to track your progress. As you outline these goals, consider your current financial situation. Factor in your income, expenses, and any debts you may have. This realistic assessment will help you align your ambitions with what's attainable given your circumstances.

Once you've established your goals, the next step is to devise a strategy for accomplishing them. For instance, if one of your goals is to eliminate student loans faster, explore various repayment strategies, such as prioritizing high-interest loans or utilizing any available loan forgiveness programs. Additionally, look into automating your finances. By setting up automatic transfers to high-interest savings accounts or debt repayment plans, you can streamline your efforts and ensure your money flows toward your goals without requiring constant oversight. This can create a sense of ease in your financial journey.

Don't forget the importance of flexibility in your goal-setting process. Life is unpredictable, and sometimes your financial priorities will shift, whether due to a new job opportunity, unexpected expenses, or personal milestones. It's crucial to periodically review and adjust your goals as needed. Celebrate your progress along the way—every small victory counts. Perhaps you've successfully saved $1,000 for your emergency fund or negotiated a raise at work. Acknowledging these achievements can fuel your motivation to keep pushing forward toward your larger financial objectives.

Finally, remember that setting financial goals is not just about numbers; it's about creating a life that aligns with your values and passions. While it's vital to focus on debt reduction and savings, also consider integrating enjoyment into your financial plan. Budgeting techniques that prioritize your personal interests and experiences can make the journey more fulfilling. When you balance your financial goals with the things you love, you'll not only work toward a secure financial future but also cultivate a lifestyle that brings you joy and satisfaction. Embrace this journey with an open heart, and watch as you transform your financial reality into one that reflects your true aspirations.

Strategies to Eliminate Your Debt and Student Loans

Creating a Debt Repayment Plan

Creating a debt repayment plan is a crucial step toward regaining control over your finances and paving the way to financial freedom. For those with low and medium incomes, the burden of debt can feel overwhelming. However, by developing a structured approach to repayment, you can break free from the cycle of debt and build a brighter future. This plan is not just about numbers; it's about creating a roadmap that aligns with your values, goals, and lifestyle.

Begin by assessing your current financial situation. List all your debts, including student loans, credit cards, and any other obligations, along with their interest rates and minimum monthly payments. This comprehensive overview provides clarity and helps you prioritize which debts to tackle first. For instance, focusing on high-interest debts can save you significant money over time. Remember, knowledge is power; understanding where you stand financially is the first step toward change.

Next, set clear, achievable repayment goals. This could be as simple as aiming to pay off a particular debt within a specific timeframe or committing to increase your monthly payments. By establishing measurable goals, you can track your progress and stay motivated. Consider using the *snowball* method, where you pay off the smallest debts first to gain momentum, or the *avalanche* method, where you tackle the highest interest debts first. Choose a strategy that resonates with you and fits your lifestyle, ensuring it feels less like a chore and more like a positive challenge.

Automating your payments is a powerful tool in your debt repayment arsenal. Set up automatic transfers to your creditors to ensure you never miss a payment, thus avoiding late fees and penalties. Many banks offer no-fee, high-interest savings accounts that can help you build an emergency fund while you pay down your debts. This dual strategy not only safeguards your financial future but also allows for a smoother repayment process. Furthermore, automate extra payments whenever possible; even small, consistent contributions can significantly reduce the total interest paid over time.

Lastly, remember that your journey to financial wellness is as much about mindset as it is about money. Celebrate your victories, no matter how small, and remain adaptable. Life is dynamic, and so are your circumstances; adjust your plan as needed. Surround yourself with supportive resources and communities, and don't hesitate to seek professional advice if necessary. With determination and a well-crafted debt repayment plan, you can transform your financial situation and ultimately achieve the freedom to enjoy life without the weight of debt holding you back.

Snowball vs. Avalanche Methods: Choosing Your Strategy

In the journey toward financial freedom, debt can often feel like an overwhelming mountain. However, the right strategy can turn that mountain into a manageable hill. Among the most effective approaches to debt repayment are the Snowball and Avalanche methods, each offering distinct advantages that resonate with different personal circumstances. Understanding these methods will empower you to take control of your financial future, eliminating debt faster and more effectively than you might have imagined.

The Snowball Method is all about motivation and momentum. This strategy encourages you to focus on paying off your smallest debts first, regardless of interest rates. By eliminating these smaller debts quickly, you gain a sense of accomplishment that fuels your drive to tackle larger debts. Imagine the feeling of crossing off those smaller bills from your list, each payment acting as a victory that propels you forward. For many, this psychological boost can be the key to staying committed. If you're someone who thrives on quick wins and needs that extra push to stay focused on long-term goals, the Snowball Method may be your ideal strategy.

Conversely, the Avalanche Method targets high-interest debts first, saving you more money in the long run. This approach prioritizes debts based on their interest rates, allowing you to pay less in interest overall. If you have a significant amount of high-interest debt, like credit card balances, this method can be particularly effective. By tackling the most costly debts first, you can reduce the overall time and money spent on repayment. For those who prefer a logical, numbers-driven approach to finances, the Avalanche Method might align better with your mindset and financial goals.

Choosing between these two strategies doesn't have to be an either-or decision; some individuals find success by combining elements of both methods. Assess your personal circumstances, including the types of debts you have and your motivation style. It's essential to consider your emotional and financial landscape when making this decision. Perhaps you start with the Snowball method for motivation and then switch to the Avalanche approach for the long-term gains. The key is to create a plan that resonates with you and keeps you engaged in your financial journey.

Ultimately, regardless of which method you choose, the most important step is to take action. Automating your payments, setting reminders, and using budgeting tools can simplify the process, allowing you to focus on what truly matters: your financial well-being. Embrace the strategy that best aligns with your personality and financial situation, and watch as you transform your debt from a source of stress into a stepping stone toward wealth and freedom. The path to financial stability is within your reach; with the right tools and mindset, you can conquer your debts and build a brighter future.

Tips for Recent Graduates on Managing Student Loans

Managing student loans can feel overwhelming, especially for recent graduates stepping into a world of financial independence. The good news is that with strategic planning and a proactive mindset, you can tackle your debt more effectively than you might think. Start by understanding the terms of your loans. Familiarize yourself with interest rates, repayment schedules, and any available forgiveness programs. Knowledge is power, and the more you know about your loans, the better equipped you'll be to manage them. This initial step lays the foundation for a successful repayment journey and empowers you to make informed decisions about your financial future.

Creating a budget tailored to your income and expenses is another essential step in managing student loans. Begin by tracking your spending to identify areas where you can cut back. Even small adjustments can free up additional funds for loan payments. Consider using budgeting apps or spreadsheets to automate this process, which can help you stay organized without feeling overwhelmed. Allocate a portion of your income specifically for loan repayment, treating it as a non-negotiable expense. By prioritizing your loans in your budget, you position yourself to make consistent payments and reduce your debt more quickly.

For those with multiple loans, consolidating or refinancing can be a game-changer. This option can simplify your payment process and potentially lower your interest rates. Research various lenders to find the best deals, and don't hesitate to ask questions to ensure you fully understand the implications of consolidation. If you're eligible, look into income-driven repayment plans that can adjust your monthly payments based on your earnings. This flexibility can be invaluable, especially during your early career when income may be inconsistent. Remember, each step you take toward managing your loans is a step toward financial freedom.

Automating your payments is another powerful strategy. Set up automatic withdrawals from your bank account for your loan payments to avoid late fees and ensure you never miss a due date. Many lenders offer a discount on interest rates for borrowers who enroll in autopay, providing an extra incentive to streamline your repayment process. Additionally, consider using high-interest savings accounts to build an emergency fund. This financial cushion can protect you from unexpected expenses and prevent you from falling behind on your loan payments.

Finally, embrace the mindset of viewing your student loans as a temporary hurdle rather than a lifelong burden. Celebrate each milestone, whether it's paying off a small loan or making an extra payment toward a larger one. Seek support from fellow graduates or financial advisors who can provide encouragement and share their own strategies. Remember that your journey to financial wellness is not just about eliminating debt but about creating a fulfilling life. By implementing these tips and maintaining a positive outlook, you can transform your relationship with student loans and pave the way for a brighter financial future.

Opening No-Fee, High-Interest Bank Accounts

Understanding High-Interest Savings Accounts

High-Interest Savings Accounts (HISAs) represent a powerful tool for individuals and families striving to build their financial futures. For those with low to medium incomes, every dollar saved can significantly impact long-term wealth. Unlike traditional savings accounts that offer minimal interest, HISAs provide an opportunity to earn more on your money, turning savings into a dynamic force working for you. By understanding the benefits and features of these accounts, you can take a crucial step toward achieving your financial goals—whether it's eliminating debt, planning for major expenses, or simply saving for a rainy day.

The primary allure of a high-interest savings account lies in its ability to maximize your savings without undue complexity. When you place your hard-earned money into these accounts, it begins to accrue interest at a higher rate than you might find at a conventional bank. This means that not only are you saving, but your money is actively growing. For the general public, especially those just starting their savings journey, this can feel like a significant step forward. Imagine watching your savings grow while you focus on your daily life—this is the essence of a HISA, providing a simple yet effective way to build a financial cushion.

Finding the right HISA comes down to knowing what to look for. Many financial institutions offer options without monthly fees, which can otherwise chip away at your savings. As you explore your choices, consider factors like the interest rate offered, minimum balance requirements, and accessibility. Some accounts allow for easy online transfers, making it simple to manage your savings while keeping your funds readily available for future needs. By prioritizing these elements, you can ensure that your savings strategy remains effective and stress-free, allowing you to concentrate on more pressing financial goals, like debt repayment or budgeting for significant life events.

Automating your contributions to a high-interest savings account is a transformative strategy that aligns perfectly with busy lifestyles. Just as many financial advisors advocate for automation in personal finance, setting up regular deposits into your HISA can help you build wealth effortlessly. By scheduling automatic transfers, you can ensure that saving becomes a seamless part of your routine, freeing up mental space to tackle other financial priorities. This hands-off approach not only simplifies saving but also instills a sense of discipline that can lead to substantial financial rewards over time.

In conclusion, embracing high-interest savings accounts is a vital step toward financial empowerment. They serve as a foundation for building an emergency fund, saving for major purchases, and even providing a buffer against unexpected expenses. By understanding the features and benefits of HISAs, actively seeking out no-fee options, and automating your savings, you can lay a solid groundwork for a prosperous financial future. The journey to financial freedom begins with informed choices, and with high-interest savings accounts, you are well on your way to transforming your financial landscape, one smart decision at a time.

Criteria for Selecting the Best Accounts

In the journey towards financial freedom, selecting the best accounts is a pivotal step that can significantly influence your overall wealth-building strategy. For individuals with low to medium incomes, every penny counts, and knowing what to look for in financial accounts can make all the difference. The right accounts can help eliminate debt more swiftly, accumulate savings without draining resources, and provide a solid foundation for future investments. By understanding the criteria for selecting the best accounts, you can streamline your finances and set yourself on a path to success.

First and foremost, prioritize accounts that align with your financial goals. Whether your aim is to pay off student loans, build an emergency fund, or save for a major life event, having the right type of account is essential. Look for high-interest savings accounts that offer no fees, as these provide a great opportunity to grow your savings without incurring unnecessary costs. When assessing these accounts, pay close attention to interest rates, minimum balance requirements, and any hidden fees that could erode your savings. Choosing accounts that support your financial aspirations will empower you to manage your money effectively and reach your goals faster.

Another critical aspect to consider is the automation features offered by financial institutions. In today's fast-paced world, automating your finances can save you time and reduce the likelihood of late fees. Seek accounts that allow for easy automation of deposits, bill payments, and transfers. This not only simplifies your financial management but also ensures that your money flows exactly where you want it to go. By implementing automation, you can focus on enjoying life while your finances work behind the scenes to support your goals, whether that means paying off debts or saving for future investments.

Moreover, effective communication with your creditors is paramount in managing accounts, especially if you encounter financial challenges. Equip yourself with scripts for avoiding late fees and negotiating better terms. Establishing a clear line of communication can lead to more favorable conditions for your accounts, giving you leverage when discussing payment plans or interest rates. Knowing what to say and how to articulate your needs can turn potential setbacks into opportunities for financial improvement, allowing you to maintain control over your financial situation.

Finally, continually educate yourself about the different financial products available in the market. The landscape of banking and investment accounts is ever-evolving, with new options emerging that could better serve your needs. Take the time to research and compare various accounts, keeping an eye out for those that offer the best benefits without compromising your hard-earned money. By staying informed and being proactive in your selection process, you will not only make sound financial decisions but also cultivate a mindset geared towards achieving your wealth-building goals. Embrace the journey of financial empowerment, and remember that the right accounts are the stepping stones to a brighter financial future.

Avoiding Bank Fees: What to Look For

Avoiding bank fees is a crucial step in streamlining your finances, especially for individuals and families on a budget. Many banks impose a variety of fees that can slowly chip away at your hard-earned savings. These fees may include monthly maintenance charges, ATM withdrawal fees, overdraft penalties, and even charges for simply maintaining a minimum balance. By becoming informed about what to look for, you can avoid these unnecessary costs and redirect your funds toward your financial goals. Remember, every dollar saved from fees is a dollar you can use toward paying off debt, building an emergency fund, or investing in your future.

Start by researching banks and credit unions that offer no-fee accounts. Many financial institutions are now competing for customers by eliminating monthly maintenance fees and providing free access to ATMs. Look for accounts that not only waive these fees but also offer high-interest rates on your savings. High-interest savings accounts can significantly boost your savings over time, allowing your money to work for you rather than being eroded by fees. Take the time to compare different institutions, as you'll often find that community banks and credit unions can provide better terms than larger banks.

Another key strategy is to read the fine print. Understanding the terms and conditions associated with your bank account can prevent unexpected charges. Some accounts may appear to be fee-free at first glance but contain hidden fees for services such as wire transfers or foreign transactions. Make sure to ask about any potential charges upfront. Don't hesitate to reach out to customer service representatives for clarification—they're there to help and can provide insights into how to avoid fees altogether.

In addition to selecting the right bank, automating your finances can play a significant role in avoiding late fees and overdraft charges. By setting up automatic transfers for your bills and savings, you ensure that payments are made on time without the risk of incurring fees. This method not only streamlines your financial management but also helps you stay on track with your budgeting goals. Consider using budgeting apps that provide reminders and alerts for upcoming bills, so you can manage your money with confidence and ease.

Finally, always be proactive in communicating with your bank. If you find yourself facing a fee, don't hesitate to call and discuss it with a representative. Many banks are willing to waive fees for loyal customers or those who explain their situation. Use effective communication techniques to express your concerns clearly and confidently. By taking these steps, you can cultivate a healthier financial lifestyle—one that prioritizes savings and minimizes unnecessary costs. Remember, every small effort adds up, and by avoiding bank fees, you are one step closer to achieving your financial dreams.

Automating Your Finances

A Step-by-Step Guide For An Average Joe

When it comes to managing finances, the average Joe often feels overwhelmed by the sheer amount of information available. However, streamlining your finances doesn't have to be complicated. This guide provides practical, step-by-step strategies tailored for those with low to medium incomes. By following these actionable insights, you can tackle debt, boost your savings, and set yourself on a path to financial independence—all while enjoying life's little pleasures.

First, let's focus on debt repayment strategies that can help you eliminate loans faster than you might think. Start by listing all your debts, including student loans, credit cards, and any other outstanding balances. Prioritize them using the avalanche or snowball method. The avalanche method involves paying off high-interest debts first, while the snowball method focuses on the smallest debts to build momentum. Choose the approach that resonates with you and set up automatic payments to ensure you never miss a due date. This simple act reduces stress and keeps your repayment journey on track.

Next, let's discuss high-interest savings accounts that won't charge you fees. Research online banks to find options that offer competitive interest rates without monthly maintenance fees. Open an account that aligns with your financial goals and set up automatic transfers from your checking account. This creates a "pay yourself first" mentality, allowing savings to grow effortlessly. Even small contributions can add up over time, creating a safety net that cushions your finances against unexpected expenses.

Automating your finances is a game-changer, especially for busy professionals. Categorize your expenses and set up automatic transfers for bills, savings, and investments. Use budgeting apps to track your spending and ensure your money is allocated where you want it. This hands-off approach allows you to focus on your career and personal life while knowing your financial goals are being actively pursued. By simplifying your financial management, you can enjoy peace of mind and clarity.

To further enhance your financial health, consider ways to save hundreds each month while still indulging in what you love. Create a budget that includes both necessities and discretionary spending. Use scripts to negotiate lower rates on bills or inquire about loyalty programs. Don't shy away from discussing your financial situation with creditors; a polite and assertive approach can often lead to waived fees or adjusted payment plans. By taking control of your expenses, you open doors to a more enjoyable lifestyle without compromising your financial goals.

Finally, as you navigate major life events like buying a car or planning a wedding, employ effective financial planning techniques. Outline a budget for these expenses well in advance, allowing you to save incrementally. Seek out community resources or workshops that offer advice on managing significant costs. Additionally, when it comes to salary negotiations, arm yourself with precise language that communicates your value to your employer. Practice these negotiation tactics to build confidence and secure the raise you deserve. By taking these steps, you'll cultivate a mindset of proactive financial management, paving the way for a future filled with opportunities and prosperity.

Tools and Apps for Financial Automation

In today's fast-paced world, managing finances can often feel overwhelming, especially for those with low to medium incomes. However, the emergence of innovative tools and apps for financial automation has transformed the landscape, making it easier than ever to take control of your financial future. These digital resources empower individuals to streamline their money management, eliminate debt, and save for significant life events without the stress that often accompanies financial planning. By embracing these tools, you can pave the way toward achieving your financial goals while still enjoying the moments that matter most.

First and foremost, debt repayment is a crucial priority for many. Apps like YNAB (You Need A Budget) and Mint offer user-friendly interfaces that help you track your spending, set budgets, and identify areas where you can cut back. With features that allow you to visualize your progress, these tools can motivate you to stick to your repayment plan. Imagine seeing your debt balance decrease month after month, fueling your commitment to becoming debt-free. Furthermore, automation features enable you to schedule payments directly from your bank account, ensuring you never miss a due date, thus avoiding those pesky late fees that can derail your progress.

For those looking to grow their savings without sacrificing their lifestyle, high-interest savings accounts are an excellent option. Online banks and financial institutions are increasingly offering no-fee, high-interest accounts that help your money work harder for you. Apps like Qapital and Digit take savings to the next level by allowing you to set specific goals, whether that's saving for a vacation or an emergency fund. These platforms use automation to analyze your spending habits and suggest small, manageable amounts to save regularly, making it easier to reach your financial objectives without feeling deprived.

Investment can seem daunting, especially for beginners, but platforms like Acorns and Betterment simplify the process. These apps automate your investments based on your financial goals and risk tolerance, allowing you to build wealth passively without needing extensive knowledge or management. By rounding up your everyday purchases and investing the spare change, you can effortlessly contribute to your future while still enjoying your current lifestyle. This hands-off approach not only demystifies investing but also encourages you to cultivate a long-term wealth-building mindset.

Lastly, for major life events like buying a home, planning a wedding or having a baby, financial automation tools can help you manage costs effectively. Budgeting apps can provide a comprehensive overview of your finances, allowing you to allocate funds efficiently for different expenses. By utilizing features that remind you of upcoming expenses and deadlines, you can navigate these significant milestones with confidence, ensuring that you stay on track without the last-minute financial panic. With the right tools in your corner, you can transform your financial landscape, eliminate debt, and save for the future—all while enjoying the life you love.

Setting Up Automatic Transfers and Payments

Setting up automatic transfers and payments is a powerful step toward achieving financial stability and peace of mind. For those with low to medium incomes, the thought of managing multiple bills and savings goals can be daunting. However, by automating these processes, you free yourself from the stress of manual management and gain more control over your financial destiny. Imagine a life where your bills are paid on time, your savings grow effortlessly, and you can focus on enjoying life rather than worrying about money.

The first step in this transformative journey is to identify your recurring expenses. These include rent or mortgage payments, utility bills, credit card payments, and any subscriptions you may have. By listing them out, you can see where your money goes each month. Once you have a clear picture, you can set up automatic payments through your bank or directly with the service providers. Most companies today offer online platforms that allow you to schedule payments in advance, ensuring you never miss a due date. This simple act not only helps you avoid late fees but also boosts your credit score over time.

Next, consider setting up automatic transfers to your savings account. Even if you can only spare a small amount each month, automating this process can lead to significant savings over time. Look for a no-fee, high-interest savings account that allows you to grow your money without draining your resources. By scheduling these transfers right after payday, you prioritize saving and create a habit that builds your financial cushion. This can be especially important for those with variable incomes, as it ensures you save consistently, regardless of fluctuations.

Automation also extends to debt repayment strategies. For recent graduates or anyone with outstanding loans, setting up automatic payments can help you tackle your debt more effectively. Consider using the snowball method—where you focus on paying off the smallest debts first—while automating payments for each account. This not only streamlines your repayment process but also gives you a sense of accomplishment as you eliminate debts one by one. Moreover, many lenders offer discounts for enrolling in automatic payments, providing an additional incentive for you to take this step.

Finally, remember that automation doesn't mean you should ignore your finances altogether. Regularly review your automated transfers and payments to ensure they still align with your financial goals. Life changes, and so should your financial strategies. By taking the time to assess your situation, you position yourself to make informed adjustments that can lead to even greater financial success. Embrace automation as a tool that empowers you to streamline your finances, achieve your goals, and ultimately, enjoy the life you envision without the constant stress of managing every detail manually.

Avoiding Late Fees

Effective Communication with Creditors

Effective communication with creditors is a vital skill that can empower you to take control of your financial situation, especially if you're navigating the challenging waters of debt. Whether you're dealing with credit card companies, student loan servicers, or any other creditors, knowing how to articulate your needs and intentions can lead to more favorable outcomes. This chapter will guide you through the process of establishing open lines of communication, which can significantly ease your financial burden and help you eliminate debt faster than you might have imagined.

The first step in effective communication is preparation. Before reaching out to a creditor, take the time to gather all relevant information, such as account numbers, outstanding balances, and any payment history that can support your case. This preparation not only boosts your confidence but also demonstrates to the creditor that you are serious about addressing your situation. When you initiate the conversation, be clear about your goals—whether it's negotiating a lower interest rate, setting up a payment plan, or discussing potential deferment options. A well-structured approach positions you as a proactive customer, increasing the chances of a positive response.

Using the right language is crucial when communicating with creditors. Aim for a tone that is both respectful and assertive. Phrases like "I would like to discuss my options" or "I appreciate any flexibility you can offer" can create an atmosphere of collaboration. Remember, creditors are often open to negotiation, particularly if they believe you are committed to repaying your debts. If you encounter resistance, don't hesitate to ask for a supervisor or someone with more authority. This persistence can often lead to better terms and solutions that align with your financial goals.

Another essential aspect is understanding your rights as a borrower. Familiarize yourself with relevant regulations, such as the Fair Debt Collection Practices Act, which protects you from unfair treatment. This knowledge empowers you to speak confidently and assertively during conversations with creditors. If a creditor is engaging in practices that feel threatening or unethical, knowing your rights allows you to advocate for yourself and seek resolution through appropriate channels. This understanding not only aids in your current situation but also builds your financial literacy for future interactions.

Finally, always follow up in writing after any significant conversation. Summarize the details of your discussion, including any agreements made, and send this to the creditor as a formal record. This not only reinforces your commitment but also serves as documentation in case of future disputes. Staying organized and proactive in your communications can significantly alleviate stress and help you stay on track with your debt repayment journey. By mastering these techniques, you can navigate the complexities of creditor relationships with confidence, ultimately paving the way toward financial freedom and a more secure future.

Scripts for Negotiating Waivers

Negotiating waivers can feel daunting, especially for individuals managing low to medium incomes. However, equipping yourself with the right scripts can transform this seemingly intimidating task into an empowering experience. Whether you're seeking waivers for late fees, service charges, or other financial penalties, clear communication is key. The following scripts are designed to help you approach these conversations with confidence, ensuring you articulate your needs effectively and increase your chances of receiving favorable outcomes.

Start by preparing your approach with a concise script that establishes your case. For example, when contacting a creditor about a late fee, consider saying, "Hello, my name is [Your Name], and I hope you can assist me with an issue regarding my account. I recently missed a payment due to [briefly explain your situation, such as unexpected expenses or illness]. I value my relationship with your company and have always aimed to maintain my account in good standing. Given these circumstances, I would appreciate your consideration in waiving the late fee this one time." This script sets a respectful tone while clearly presenting your request.

When negotiating for a waiver on service charges or other fees, maintain a focus on your loyalty and history with the institution. A script like, "Hi, this is [Your Name]. I've been a customer for [duration of time] and have always appreciated the service I receive. I noticed a recent charge on my account that I would like to discuss. Could we review this together? I would be grateful if you could consider waiving it, given my longstanding relationship with your company." This approach emphasizes your loyalty, which can encourage the representative to assist you further.

If you encounter resistance, it's vital to remain calm and persistent. You can try a follow-up script: "I understand your policies are in place for a reason, and I appreciate your position. However, I would like to ask if there is any flexibility regarding my situation. Is there a supervisor I could speak with who might have the authority to grant my request?" This shows respect for the representative's role while also advocating for your needs. Remember, persistence can pay off, and often, a different voice may have the power to help.

In situations where you are negotiating waivers for academic-related fees, such as late tuition payments, modify your script to reflect your educational commitment: "Hello, I'm [Your Name], a student at [Your Institution]. I'm reaching out to discuss a late fee that was applied to my account. Due to unforeseen circumstances, I was unable to make my payment on time. I am dedicated to my education and would greatly appreciate your consideration in waiving this fee, as it would significantly help me continue my studies without financial strain." This tailored approach reflects your commitment to your education and appeals to the institution's desire to support students.

Using these scripts as a foundation, remember that negotiation is a skill that can be developed over time. Each conversation is an opportunity to practice assertiveness and build financial resilience. With the right preparation and mindset, you can navigate these discussions successfully, freeing up resources that can be better directed towards your financial goals. Embrace the process of negotiation; it's a step toward taking control of your finances and paving the way to a more secure and prosperous future.

Creating Reminders and Alerts

Creating reminders and alerts is a powerful yet often overlooked strategy for managing your finances efficiently. In the fast-paced world we live in, it's easy to lose track of due dates for bills, loan payments, or even savings contributions. Setting up reminders and alerts can serve as your personal financial assistant, ensuring that you stay on top of your obligations while also allowing you to make consistent progress toward your financial goals. This simple step can prevent late fees from piling up and help you maintain a healthy credit score, setting the stage for a brighter financial future.

Imagine waking up each day knowing that your finances are organized and that you won't miss a payment or an opportunity to save. By using calendar apps or dedicated financial management tools, you can schedule reminders for all your critical deadlines.

Whether it's the day your student loan payment is due or the moment your paycheck arrives, these alerts can empower you to take action. This proactive approach not only minimizes stress but also allows you to allocate your resources more effectively, paving the way for faster debt elimination and smarter savings strategies.

In addition to payment reminders, alerts can be utilized to track your progress on savings goals. For instance, if you're aiming to save for a major life event like buying a car or planning a wedding, set alerts for when you've reached specific milestones. This not only keeps you accountable but also provides motivation as you see how close you are to achieving your objectives. By integrating these reminders into your daily routine, you transform your financial aspirations from distant dreams into achievable realities.

Moreover, the art of creating alerts doesn't stop at just payments and savings. You can also set reminders for evaluating your financial products, like checking for no-fee high-interest savings accounts or reviewing your investment strategy. Regularly revisiting these aspects of your finances can lead to significant savings and better returns over time. By making a habit of checking in on your financial health, you're actively participating in your wealth-building journey while keeping yourself informed and engaged.

Lastly, consider the power of communication in your financial management. Setting reminders to reach out to creditors about potential late fees or to negotiate a raise at work can open doors you didn't know existed. Scripts can be prepared in advance, and alerts can prompt you to take these essential steps toward financial empowerment. In this way, reminders not only keep you organized but also encourage you to take decisive actions that can lead to substantial financial benefits. Embrace the simplicity of reminders and alerts, and watch as they transform your financial landscape, guiding you toward the wealth and freedom you deserve.

Budgeting Techniques for Enjoyment

The Balance Between Saving and Enjoying Life

The journey toward financial stability is often painted as a strict regimen of saving and sacrificing. Yet, the truth is that life is meant to be enjoyed, even while you're working to eliminate debt or build a solid financial foundation. The balance between saving and enjoying life is not merely a tightrope walk; it can be a harmonious dance where both can coexist. This balance is essential for low and medium-income earners who seek to streamline their finances without compromising their quality of life. It's about creating a financial plan that allows you to savor the small joys while systematically working toward your financial goals.

Emphasizing enjoyment doesn't mean abandoning your financial responsibilities. Instead, it means redefining what enjoyment looks like within your current means. Consider allocating a portion of your budget for experiences and activities that bring you joy—whether it's a weekly coffee ritual with friends or a monthly outing to a local event. By consciously carving out space for enjoyment, you can prevent the feeling of deprivation that often comes with aggressive saving strategies. This approach not only enhances your quality of life but also reinforces your commitment to your financial goals, as you allow yourself to enjoy the journey rather than viewing it solely as a grind.

When it comes to automating your finances, the key is to set up systems that facilitate both saving and spending in a way that feels effortless. Utilize high-interest savings accounts that don't drain your resources, ensuring that your money grows while you enjoy life. Automating your savings can be a game-changer—allocating a percentage of your income to savings and investments before you even see it in your checking account makes it easier to stick to your financial plan. This strategy allows you to enjoy your hard-earned money without the guilt of overspending, as you know your savings are steadily increasing in the background.

As you navigate major expenses—like buying a car, planning a wedding, or raising children—embracing a balanced approach becomes even more critical. It's essential to be realistic about your financial capacity while also being open to creative solutions that can enhance your experience. For instance, negotiating for better terms on loans or seeking out budget-friendly alternatives can help you manage these significant costs without sacrificing the joy associated with these life events. By setting clear priorities and being willing to explore alternative options, you can enjoy these milestones without the weight of financial stress.

Lastly, remember that financial well-being is not a destination but an ongoing journey. As you work towards eliminating debt and building a savings cushion, allow yourself the grace to indulge in life's pleasures along the way. Celebrate small victories, whether it's paying off a loan or successfully sticking to your budget for the month. By maintaining this balance between saving and enjoying, you create a sustainable financial lifestyle that not only secures your future but also enriches your present. Embrace the journey, and let it empower you to live fully while you build the wealth you deserve.

Creating a Budget That Works for You

Creating a budget that works for you is not just about numbers—it's about reclaiming your financial freedom and empowering yourself to make the most of your hard-earned income. For those navigating the challenges of low and medium incomes, a well-crafted budget can serve as a powerful tool to eliminate debt, save for the future, and still enjoy life's little pleasures. By understanding your financial landscape and tailoring a budget that reflects your unique needs and aspirations, you can transform your financial situation from one of struggle to one of opportunity.

Start by assessing your current financial situation. Gather all your income sources and expenses, both fixed and variable. It's essential to have a clear picture of where your money is going each month. Documenting these figures will not only identify areas where you might be overspending but also highlight opportunities for saving. Consider using budgeting apps or simple spreadsheets to track your spending effortlessly. This initial step lays the foundation for a budget that allows you to prioritize debt repayment while ensuring you allocate funds for savings and enjoyment.

Once you have a handle on your finances, it's time to set clear, realistic goals. Whether you're aiming to pay off student loans, save for a down payment on a house, or build an emergency fund, having specific goals will keep you motivated and focused. Break down these goals into manageable milestones. For instance, if you want to eliminate credit card debt, establish a target repayment amount that fits within your budget each month. Celebrate small victories along the way, as these moments of success will inspire you to continue making progress.

Next, embrace the power of automation. By setting up automatic transfers to your savings and debt repayment accounts, you can streamline your finances and ensure that your money is working for you without constant oversight. This technique not only helps you avoid late fees but also fosters a sense of discipline in your financial habits. Automating your budget is like setting your financial future on autopilot; it allows you to focus on enjoying life while your money is directed where it needs to go.

Finally, remember that budgeting is a dynamic process. Life changes, and so do your financial needs and goals. Regularly review and adjust your budget to accommodate shifts in your circumstances or priorities. This flexibility will enable you to maintain balance in your life—ensuring that you can address major expenses, tackle debt, and enjoy the things you love. With a budget that truly works for you, financial freedom is not just a dream; it's a tangible, achievable reality. Embrace this journey, and let your budget be the roadmap that guides you toward a brighter financial future.

Cutting Costs Without Sacrificing Fun

Cutting costs while still having fun may seem like a daunting challenge, especially for those navigating the complexities of low and medium incomes. However, it's entirely possible to enjoy life without breaking the bank or sacrificing your happiness. The key lies in reimagining your approach to spending. By prioritizing experiences that bring you joy and seeking out cost-effective alternatives, you can create a lifestyle that is both fulfilling and financially sustainable. This shift in perspective can empower you to embrace financial freedom while enjoying the moments that matter most.

To begin your journey toward cost-cutting without sacrificing fun, evaluate your current expenses and identify areas where you can make adjustments. Start by scrutinizing your discretionary spending—dining out, entertainment, and shopping often take a sizable portion of your budget. Instead of cutting these activities entirely, look for creative alternatives. Consider hosting potluck dinners with friends instead of going out, or exploring free community events that offer enjoyable experiences without the hefty price tag. By cultivating a mindset of resourcefulness, you can find joy in activities that enrich your life while keeping your finances in check.

Another effective strategy is to automate your finances to streamline your savings and spending. Set up a high-interest savings account that allows you to earn money on your savings without incurring fees. Automate transfers to this account to build your savings effortlessly, creating a cushion for unexpected expenses or future enjoyment. Furthermore, by allocating a set percentage of your income to fun activities, you can enjoy guilt-free spending while remaining committed to your financial goals. This balance is crucial for maintaining motivation on your journey toward wealth-building.

Negotiating expenses can also dramatically reduce costs. Whether you're looking to lower your bills or negotiate a raise at work, mastering the language of effective communication can lead to substantial savings. Use scripts to approach creditors and request lower rates or payment plans that suit your budget. When discussing salary increases, articulate your value clearly and confidently. These conversations can lead to unexpected financial benefits, allowing you to maintain a lifestyle that supports your happiness and well-being.

Lastly, embrace lifestyle adjustments that support both your enjoyment and your financial goals. This may involve rethinking your approach to entertainment or travel. Instead of lavish vacations, explore local adventures or staycations that can provide rich experiences without high costs. By integrating these practical strategies into your life, you can successfully cut costs without sacrificing the fun. Remember, financial well-being doesn't have to mean a life devoid of joy. With careful planning and a positive mindset, you can create a life full of memorable experiences while also paving the way toward a financially secure future.

Simplifying Investment Strategies

Introduction to Passive Investment

In today's fast-paced world, many individuals find themselves overwhelmed by the complexities of managing their finances. For those in the low to medium income brackets, the prospect of building wealth can feel daunting, especially when faced with the pressures of debt and unexpected expenses. However, passive investment strategies offer a beacon of hope for those looking to streamline their financial journey. By adopting a hands-off approach to investing, anyone can begin to cultivate wealth over time without the need for extensive financial knowledge or constant oversight.

Passive investment is rooted in the philosophy of letting your money work for you while you focus on your everyday life. Unlike active investing, which requires frequent trading and a deep understanding of market trends, passive investing allows individuals to take a more relaxed approach. This means investing in diversified portfolios, such as index funds or exchange-traded funds (ETFs), that mirror the performance of the market. By doing so, you not only reduce the stress associated with daily market fluctuations but also position yourself for long-term growth with minimal effort.

One of the most significant advantages of passive investing is its accessibility. You don't need to be a financial expert to get started; with the right tools and resources, anyone can set up a passive investment strategy. Imagine a scenario where, after paying off debts and setting aside emergency savings, you allocate a small portion of your income each month to a well-chosen investment account. Over time, even small contributions can compound significantly, leading to a comfortable nest egg that supports your future goals, whether that's buying a home, funding your child's education, or enjoying well-deserved vacations.

Moreover, passive investment strategies align perfectly with the principles of automating your finances. By setting up automatic contributions to your investment accounts, you remove the temptation to spend that money elsewhere. This process not only helps you stay disciplined in your savings plan but also allows your investments to grow without requiring constant attention. Over time, this can lead to a substantial increase in your financial security and freedom, allowing you to focus on living your life to the fullest.

In conclusion, passive investment is not just a strategy; it's a mindset shift toward achieving financial independence with ease and confidence. By incorporating this approach into your financial planning, you can simplify wealth building and ensure that your hard-earned money continues to work for you, even when you're not actively managing it. Embrace the journey of passive investing and watch as your financial landscape transforms, paving the way for a brighter, more secure future.

Understanding Index Funds and ETFs

In the pursuit of financial stability and wealth growth, understanding the tools available to you is crucial. Among these tools, index funds and exchange-traded funds (ETFs) stand out as accessible and effective investment options for individuals with low to medium incomes. These investment vehicles allow you to participate in the stock market without needing extensive knowledge or a significant initial investment. They embody the idea that anyone, regardless of their financial background, can make their money work for them.

Index funds, in essence, are mutual funds designed to replicate the performance of a specific market index, such as the S&P 500. This means that when you invest in an index fund, you are essentially buying a small piece of many companies within that index, diversifying your investment with minimal effort. For those managing debt or student loans, investing in index funds can be a strategic way to grow wealth over time, allowing you to set aside a portion of your income while still working toward eliminating your financial burdens. The beauty of index funds lies in their low fees and passive management style, making them ideal for beginners looking to streamline their financial journey.

ETFs, on the other hand, offer similar benefits but come with unique features that may appeal to various investors. Like index funds, ETFs track a specific index, but they trade on stock exchanges like individual stocks, allowing for greater flexibility. This means you can buy and sell shares throughout the day, providing you with more control over your investments. For those who are busy professionals or juggling multiple financial priorities, ETFs can be an excellent way to automate your wealth-building strategy, as you can set up automatic contributions and let your investments grow without constant oversight.

Both index funds and ETFs are designed for long-term investors who seek to build wealth steadily rather than chase short-term gains. This aligns perfectly with the principles of automating your finances. By setting up automatic investments into these funds, you can ensure your money is consistently working for you, regardless of your current financial situation. This hands-off approach not only reduces the temptation to spend but also helps you stay focused on your long-term goals, whether it's paying off debt, saving for a home, or building an emergency fund.

Incorporating index funds and ETFs into your financial strategy is not just about investing; it's about adopting a mindset that prioritizes growth and stability. As you explore these investment options, remember that every small step counts. Start with what you can afford, automate your contributions, and watch your investments flourish over time. With the right knowledge and tools, you can pave the way toward a more secure financial future, transforming your dreams of wealth into a tangible reality. Embrace this journey, knowing that you are not alone, and that every effort you make brings you closer to financial freedom.

Building a Portfolio That Outperforms Advisors

Building a portfolio that outperforms advisors is not just a dream; it's an achievable reality for anyone willing to take charge of their financial future. For individuals with low and medium incomes, the idea of creating a robust investment portfolio can seem daunting, especially when faced with the complexities of financial markets and the allure of professional advisors. However, the truth is that with the right strategies and a commitment to learning, you can build a wealth-generating portfolio that meets your needs and goals without relying solely on external experts.

To begin, it's essential to understand the power of automation in managing your investments. Automating your finances allows you to consistently contribute to your portfolio without the stress of remembering to make transactions. By setting up automatic transfers to investment accounts, you can ensure that a portion of your income is consistently working for you. This method not only helps in building wealth over time but also takes advantage of dollar-cost averaging, which can reduce the impact of market volatility on your investments. When you pay yourself first and automate your wealth-building efforts, you create a solid foundation for financial growth.

Next, prioritize simplicity in your investment choices. Many people believe that successful investing requires an intricate understanding of the stock market or an extensive education in finance. In reality, a simple, hands-off investment strategy can yield impressive results. Consider low-cost index funds or exchange-traded funds (ETFs) that track market performance rather than trying to pick individual stocks. These options often outperform actively managed funds—commonly recommended by financial advisors—due to lower fees and the tendency of the market to rise over time. By focusing on simplicity and consistency, you position yourself to outperform those who rely heavily on advisor recommendations.

Debt management is another crucial element in building a portfolio that works for you. High-interest debts can severely hinder your ability to invest effectively. By implementing strategies to eliminate debt quickly, such as the snowball or avalanche methods, you will free up more funds to allocate towards your investment portfolio. Additionally, consider negotiating lower interest rates or exploring consolidation options. Once your debt is under control, you'll find a renewed ability to invest in your future, allowing your portfolio to flourish without the weight of financial burdens.

Lastly, embrace a mindset of continuous learning and adaptation. The financial landscape is always evolving, and staying informed about market trends, new investment vehicles, and effective saving strategies will empower you to make informed decisions. Utilize online resources, attend workshops, or read books that resonate with your financial journey. By combining your knowledge with a disciplined investment approach, you can create a portfolio that not only meets but exceeds the performance of traditional financial advisors. Remember, your financial success is within reach; it's time to take the reins and build a wealth portfolio that works tirelessly for you.

Managing Major Expenses with Ease

Financial Planning for Buying a Car

Financial planning for purchasing a car is not just about crunching numbers; it's about strategically aligning your goals and aspirations with your everyday financial realities. For those in the low to medium income brackets, the prospect of buying a car can often feel overwhelming, especially with the burdens of debt and student loans weighing heavily on your shoulders. However, with a well-thought-out plan, you can take control of your finances and make the dream of car ownership a reality. This subchapter will guide you through the essential steps to ensure that buying a car is a positive investment, rather than a source of financial stress.

Begin by assessing your current financial situation. Take a close look at your income, expenses, and any existing debts. Understanding your cash flow will help you determine how much you can realistically allocate toward a car payment without jeopardizing your other financial commitments. A practical approach is to create a budget that prioritizes your essential expenses while carving out room for saving toward your car purchase. Aim to set aside a specific amount each month that will build your down payment, which will not only reduce your monthly payments but also help you avoid high-interest financing options that can lead to long-term debt.

Next, consider the total cost of ownership when selecting a vehicle. The purchase price is only one aspect; think about insurance, maintenance, fuel, and registration fees as well. Research vehicles that fit within your budget and also have a reputation for reliability and low maintenance costs. Online resources and community forums can be invaluable for uncovering insights on the best cars for your financial situation. By choosing a car that aligns with your budget both at the point of purchase and in ongoing expenses, you can enjoy the benefits of car ownership without compromising your financial health.

Another essential component of financial planning for buying a car is exploring your financing options carefully. If you're not purchasing outright, shop around for loans to find the best interest rates and terms available to you. Many credit unions offer favorable rates, especially for members, so consider joining one if you haven't already. Automate your savings for a down payment, and consider using tools that enable you to monitor your credit score, which can impact your financing options. A higher credit score may qualify you for lower interest rates, saving you significant money in the long run.

Finally, be prepared to negotiate, whether you're dealing with a sales representative or a bank. Equip yourself with knowledge about the car's market value and be ready to ask for better terms or prices. Effective communication can lead to savings that might seem unreachable at first. Remember, buying a car is not just a transaction; it's a step toward greater freedom and mobility. With diligent financial planning, you can turn this aspiration into a reality, paving the way for a more prosperous and enjoyable life. Embrace the journey, and let the art of financial planning guide you to the car of your dreams without compromising your financial future.

Budgeting for a Home Purchase

Budgeting for a home purchase is a pivotal step in the journey toward financial stability and personal fulfillment. For many individuals and families with low to medium incomes, the dream of homeownership can feel like a distant reality. However, with the right strategies and a clear plan, that dream can transform into a tangible achievement. By understanding the importance of budgeting, you can pave the way to a future where you own your home and enjoy the financial freedom that comes with it.

The first step in budgeting for a home purchase is to create a comprehensive financial overview. Start by assessing your current income, expenses, and any existing debt. This will give you a clearer picture of your financial health. Identify areas where you can cut back on non-essential expenses—whether it's dining out less frequently or canceling subscriptions you rarely use. By reallocating these funds toward your home savings, you'll begin to inch closer to that down payment. Remember, every little bit counts, and small sacrifices today can lead to significant gains tomorrow.

Next, it's essential to establish a realistic savings goal for your down payment. A common benchmark is 20% of the home's purchase price, but many programs allow for lower down payments. Consider your desired home price and work backwards to define how much you need to save each month. Utilize high-interest savings accounts, preferably no-fee options, to maximize your savings without draining your finances. Automating your savings can also streamline this process; set up a direct deposit from your paycheck into your savings account, ensuring that you're consistently working towards your goal without the temptation to spend that money elsewhere.

As you progress in your home-buying journey, don't forget to factor in additional costs beyond the down payment. Closing costs, home inspections, and moving expenses can add up quickly. Creating a detailed budget that includes these expenses will help you avoid any financial surprises. Additionally, consider the long-term costs of homeownership, such as maintenance, property taxes, and insurance. By preparing for these ongoing expenses, you can ensure that your new home fits comfortably within your overall financial strategy.

Finally, remember that budgeting for a home purchase is not just about numbers; it's about building a future. The sacrifices you make today, the money you save, and the strategic planning you undertake are all investments in your life's aspirations. Embrace this journey as an opportunity to cultivate discipline and resilience—qualities that will serve you well in all areas of your financial life.
Homeownership is within reach, and with a solid budget, you can turn that dream into reality, creating a space that reflects your values and aspirations while securing your financial future.

Preparing for Major Life Events: Weddings and Children

Preparing for significant life events such as weddings and the arrival of children can evoke a whirlwind of emotions, from excitement to anxiety. For individuals and families with low to medium incomes, the prospect of managing these milestones can feel overwhelming, particularly when trying to maintain financial stability. However, with the right strategies in place, you can navigate these moments with confidence, ensuring that your dreams do not become burdens. This subchapter will guide you through practical steps to prepare financially for these transformative events, allowing you to embrace the joy they bring while minimizing stress.

The first step in preparing for a wedding or the arrival of a child is to establish a clear budget. By setting a realistic spending plan, you can allocate funds without derailing your financial goals. Start by breaking down the costs associated with each event. For weddings, consider expenses like venue, catering, attire, and photography. For new parents, factor in essentials such as prenatal care, baby supplies, and potential childcare. Utilize budgeting tools or apps to track your progress, ensuring every dollar is accounted for. This proactive approach not only helps you avoid overspending but also empowers you to make informed decisions that align with your financial situation.

Once you have a budget in place, explore creative ways to save on these expenses. For weddings, consider hosting a smaller gathering or opting for off-peak dates to reduce costs. DIY elements, such as invitations or decorations, can infuse personal touches while saving you money. When preparing for a child, take advantage of community resources, such as second-hand marketplaces, parenting groups, and local charities that offer baby essentials. These strategies can significantly lessen the financial burden, allowing you to invest the saved funds into your future, whether that's paying down debt or starting a savings account.

Automating your finances can be a game changer when preparing for significant life events. Set up automatic transfers to a dedicated savings account specifically for wedding or baby-related expenses. This method ensures that you consistently allocate funds toward your goals without the temptation to spend. Additionally, consider automating bill payments to avoid late fees, giving you peace of mind and freeing up your mental space for more joyful preparations. By establishing these automated systems, you create a hands-off approach to financial management that allows you to focus on what truly matters during these exciting times.

As you prepare for a wedding or the arrival of a child, it's essential to communicate openly with your partner about finances. Discuss your financial goals, priorities, and any concerns you may have. This conversation fosters a sense of teamwork and shared responsibility, ensuring that both of you are on the same page. Additionally, consider seeking advice from financial professionals or utilizing online resources tailored to your situation. Understanding the financial implications of these life events can empower you to make better choices, ensuring that you embark on your new journey with a solid financial foundation.

In conclusion, while weddings and the arrival of children are joyous occasions, they come with their own set of financial challenges. By establishing a budget, exploring cost-saving strategies, automating your finances, and fostering open communication, you can prepare for these milestones without compromising your financial well-being. Embrace the excitement of these life events with the knowledge that you have laid the groundwork for a secure future. Remember, preparing for major life changes is not just about managing expenses; it is about creating a life filled with love, joy, and financial peace.

Negotiating a Substantial Raise

Preparing for the Conversation

Preparing for the conversation about your finances, especially when it comes to managing debt, maximizing savings, and negotiating better terms, is essential for anyone looking to streamline their financial situation. The journey towards financial empowerment begins with understanding the landscape you're navigating. Whether you're facing student loans or trying to find the best high-interest savings accounts, preparation is key. The right mindset and a solid plan can transform daunting discussions into opportunities for growth and relief.

Start by gathering all relevant information about your current financial obligations. Know your debts, interest rates, and monthly payments by heart. This foundational knowledge not only empowers you but also boosts your confidence during discussions with creditors or financial institutions. Prepare a list of questions or points you want to address. This could include concerns about late fees, options for consolidating debt, or inquiries about potential savings accounts with no associated fees. The more informed you are, the more effectively you can advocate for your financial future.

Next, consider the emotional aspect of these conversations. Financial discussions can often feel intimidating, particularly if you're dealing with overwhelming debt or strict budgets. Approach these talks with a positive mindset. Visualize the benefits that will result from your efforts, such as reduced stress, increased savings, and a clearer path to financial freedom. Practicing positive affirmations and visualizing a successful outcome can help reduce anxiety and prepare you to engage constructively with others.

Role-play your conversations ahead of time. Whether it's negotiating a raise with your employer or discussing repayment options with a creditor, practicing your approach can significantly enhance your confidence. Use specific scripts that outline what you want to convey, and rehearse these with a friend or family member. This preparation allows you to refine your language, ensuring you communicate your points clearly and assertively. When the moment comes to engage in these crucial conversations, you'll be ready to articulate your needs and desires with clarity.

Finally, remember that these conversations are not just about financial figures; they are also about building relationships. Approach each discussion with respect and openness. Acknowledge the perspectives of the other parties involved, whether they are creditors, bank representatives, or employers. This respectful approach can foster collaboration, making it easier to reach mutually beneficial agreements. As you prepare for these financial discussions, embrace the belief that you deserve financial well-being and are capable of achieving it through careful planning and proactive communication. Your journey to automated wealth begins with these empowering conversations.

The Language That Works: Key Phrases and Techniques

In the journey toward financial freedom, the language we use can be a powerful tool. The right phrases and techniques not only help clarify our intentions but also empower us to take control of our financial situation. This section focuses on equipping you with key phrases and strategies that resonate with lenders, employers, and financial institutions, ultimately enabling you to streamline your wealth-building efforts. Embracing this language transforms daunting financial tasks into manageable steps, setting you on a path to achieving your goals more swiftly than you ever imagined.

When it comes to negotiating debt repayment options, confidence is key. Using phrases like "I'd like to discuss potential alternatives for my debt repayment" can open the door to constructive conversations with creditors. This simple yet effective approach encourages dialogue about flexible repayment plans or reduced interest rates, potentially saving you hundreds or even thousands of dollars. For recent graduates grappling with student loans, framing your situation positively—such as expressing a commitment to repay while seeking manageable terms—can foster goodwill and lead to better outcomes.

In the realm of banking, the language you employ can significantly affect your financial trajectory. When approaching potential banks for high-interest savings accounts, consider asking, "What options do you have that offer the best interest rates with no fees?" This direct inquiry not only reflects your knowledge but also encourages financial institutions to present their best offerings. By knowing what to ask, you position yourself as a savvy consumer, capable of maximizing your savings without incurring unnecessary costs—a crucial step in automating your finances effectively.

To avoid late fees, having a clear script can make all the difference. Start with a straightforward approach: "I'd like to discuss my recent payment and see if there's a way to avoid the late fee." This pragmatic language communicates your desire to resolve the issue amicably while emphasizing your commitment to rectifying the situation. By taking this proactive stance, you not only mitigate immediate costs but also build a reputation as a responsible borrower, paving the way for more favorable terms in future financial dealings.

Lastly, mastering the art of negotiation in your professional life is essential for boosting your income and achieving financial stability. When discussing salary increases, use phrases like, "Based on my contributions to the team and the market standards, I believe a review of my compensation is warranted." This assertive yet respectful language emphasizes your value and sets the stage for a productive conversation. By effectively communicating your worth, you empower yourself to unlock the financial potential that lies within your career, ultimately contributing to a more prosperous future. Embrace these techniques, and watch as they transform your financial landscape, leading you closer to the wealth you deserve.

Following Up After the Negotiation

Following up after a negotiation is a critical step that many overlook, yet it can significantly impact your financial journey. Whether you've just negotiated a raise at work, a better interest rate on your loans, or a favorable payment plan, the follow-up is your opportunity to solidify the gains you've made. It's a chance to reinforce your commitment, express gratitude, and ensure that all parties are on the same page. Understanding how to navigate this phase can help you maintain the momentum you've built during the negotiation process and set the stage for future financial successes.

Start with a thank-you note. A simple, heartfelt expression of gratitude can go a long way in establishing rapport and goodwill. Whether your negotiation was with your employer, a lender, or a service provider, acknowledging their time and consideration demonstrates professionalism and respect. This small gesture not only strengthens your relationship but also keeps the lines of communication open for any future discussions. Remember, building strong connections can lead to better opportunities down the line, whether it's a promotion, a loan adjustment, or even referrals to beneficial resources.

Next, clarify any agreements made during the negotiation. If you discussed specific terms or timelines, reiterate them in your follow-up communication. This not only shows your attentiveness but also ensures that everyone has a clear understanding of the outcomes. A well-structured follow-up can help prevent misunderstandings and create a foundation of trust. It's also a good time to ask any lingering questions you might have about the details of the agreement, ensuring that you are fully informed as you move forward.

Don't forget to outline the next steps. If there are actions required from either party, clearly state what those are and when they should be completed. By doing so, you demonstrate your proactive approach to managing your finances. This is particularly important when applying the strategies discussed in this book, such as implementing debt repayment plans or automating your savings. Keeping everyone accountable fosters a sense of partnership, reinforcing the idea that you are working together toward mutual goals.

Finally, view this follow-up as part of an ongoing dialogue. Your financial journey is not a one-time event but a continuous process. Use this opportunity to express your interest in maintaining regular contact, whether through scheduled check-ins or updates on your progress. This not only keeps your financial goals at the forefront but also allows you to share successes and challenges along the way. By treating follow-ups as an integral part of your strategy, you empower yourself to navigate your financial landscape more effectively, open doors for new opportunities, and ultimately transform your wealth-building journey into a more manageable and rewarding experience.

Chapter 10: Building an Emergency Savings Fund

Building an Emergency Savings Fund

The Importance of a Safety Net

In today's uncertain economic landscape, building a safety net is not just a luxury; it's a necessity. For individuals and families living on low to medium incomes, the idea of financial security can feel like a distant dream. However, having a robust safety net allows you to navigate unexpected challenges with confidence. Whether it's an unforeseen medical expense, a job loss, or a sudden need for car repairs, a safety net empowers you to face these hurdles without derailing your financial progress. This subchapter will explore the importance of creating and maintaining a safety net, providing practical strategies that align perfectly with your financial journey.

Establishing a safety net begins with understanding the core components of financial security. At its essence, a safety net involves having savings set aside that can cover three to six months of living expenses. This cushion not only protects you from financial emergencies but also alleviates the stress that often accompanies financial instability. For those burdened with student loans or credit card debt, the thought of saving might seem daunting. Yet, even small, consistent contributions to a high-interest, no-fee savings account can lead to significant growth over time. By prioritizing this savings habit, you're not just preparing for emergencies; you're investing in your peace of mind.

Moreover, a safety net provides the freedom to make better choices during challenging times. When you're unprepared for financial emergencies, you may be forced to rely on high-interest loans or credit cards, trapping you in a cycle of debt. Conversely, having savings enables you to resist the temptation of quick fixes that could worsen your financial situation. You'll be able to approach life's hurdles with a clear mind and a strategic plan. This is especially relevant for young graduates navigating the complexities of student debt. By establishing an emergency fund, recent graduates can mitigate the risks associated with their financial obligations while still enjoying life's experiences.

Implementing effective budgeting techniques can significantly enhance your ability to build a safety net. Start by identifying areas where you can trim expenses without sacrificing enjoyment. This can involve simple lifestyle adjustments or utilizing budgeting apps that automate your tracking process. By allocating a portion of your income directly to an emergency fund, you can gradually build your safety net without feeling overwhelmed. Remember, the goal is not to eliminate all pleasures from your life but to strike a balance that allows you to enjoy your current lifestyle while securing your financial future.

Finally, the journey to building a safety net is not just about saving money; it's about cultivating a mindset of resilience and preparedness. It's about understanding that life will throw curveballs, but you are equipped to handle them. Engage in conversations about financial wellness, seek advice from trusted sources, and share your goals with supportive friends or family. The more you surround yourself with positive influences, the more empowered you will feel to take control of your finances. By prioritizing a safety net, you are investing in your future and creating a foundation that supports your aspirations, transforming the way you approach both challenges and opportunities in your financial life.

Strategies for Building Savings Without Stress

Building savings can often feel like an overwhelming task, especially for those managing low to medium incomes. However, the journey to financial security doesn't have to be stressful. By adopting simple, effective strategies, you can cultivate a savings habit that not only shields you from unexpected expenses but also enhances your overall quality of life. The key lies in creating a system that works for you, allowing your savings to grow effortlessly as you focus on enjoying the present.

One of the most powerful tools at your disposal is automation. By setting up automatic transfers from your checking account to a high-interest savings account, you can make saving a seamless part of your financial routine. This method not only ensures that you consistently contribute to your savings but also removes the temptation to spend that money. Look for no-fee, high-interest accounts that can significantly boost your savings without the burden of extra costs. This way, your money works for you, helping you accumulate wealth over time without additional stress.

In addition to automation, consider the impact of small lifestyle adjustments on your savings. Cutting back on unnecessary expenses can lead to significant savings without sacrificing the things you love. For example, cooking at home more often, canceling unused subscriptions, or finding free or low-cost entertainment options can add up quickly. By creating a budget that prioritizes your financial goals while still allowing for enjoyment, you can strike a balance that keeps you motivated and engaged in your savings journey.

For those facing debt, especially recent graduates, effective debt repayment strategies can free up additional funds for savings. Prioritize high-interest debts and consider consolidating loans to lower your interest rates. Implementing a debt snowball method, where you pay off the smallest debts first, can create a sense of accomplishment that fuels your motivation to save. The sooner you tackle your debts, the quicker you'll have the flexibility to redirect those funds into savings, building a safety net that brings peace of mind.

Lastly, don't underestimate the power of negotiation in your financial life. Whether it's seeking a raise at work or negotiating better terms on your bills, effective communication can lead to significant financial improvements. Equip yourself with the right language and scripts to advocate for your worth, and watch as your income grows. Each additional dollar earned can be funneled directly into your savings, propelling you closer to your financial goals. With these strategies in place, building savings becomes not just a possibility but a stress-free reality.

Automating Your Emergency Fund Contributions

Automating your emergency fund contributions is a powerful step toward achieving financial security, especially for those navigating the challenges of low and medium incomes. Life is unpredictable, and having a financial safety net can provide peace of mind during turbulent times. By setting up automatic contributions to your emergency fund, you can ensure that you are proactively preparing for the unexpected, without the stress of having to remember to do it manually each month. This simple adjustment to your financial routine can create a sense of control over your finances, allowing you to focus on building your wealth and enjoying life.

To get started, it's essential to establish a dedicated high-interest savings account specifically for your emergency fund. Unlike traditional savings accounts that may offer little to no interest, a high-interest option allows your savings to grow over time, providing a greater cushion for emergencies. Research no-fee accounts that will not drain your savings through hidden charges. This step not only maximizes your contributions but also ensures that you can make the most of your hard-earned money. Once you've found the right account, you can easily set up automated transfers from your primary checking account.

Next, determine a realistic monthly contribution amount that aligns with your budget. This could be a specific dollar amount or a percentage of your income. The key is to choose an amount that feels manageable so that you won't be tempted to skip a contribution. You might start small; even setting aside $25 a month can lead to significant savings over time. By automating this process, you are effectively "paying yourself first," making saving a priority rather than an afterthought. This consistent behavior fosters a sense of achievement as you watch your emergency fund grow steadily.

As you automate your contributions, remember that flexibility is essential. Life circumstances may change, and so may your financial situation. It's important to regularly review and adjust your contributions based on your income fluctuations or changes in your expenses. This adaptive approach ensures that your emergency fund remains a priority, regardless of external factors. You can also consider increasing your contribution during times of financial stability, such as after receiving a raise or bonus, to accelerate your savings goal.

Lastly, celebrate your progress. Each time you reach a new milestone in your emergency fund, take a moment to acknowledge your hard work and dedication. This positive reinforcement encourages the continuation of your saving habits and elevates your financial confidence. Automating your emergency fund contributions is not just about saving money; it's about cultivating a mindset of financial empowerment and resilience. By taking these steps, you are not only building a safety net but also laying the groundwork for a more secure and fulfilling future.

Lifestyle Adjustments for Debt Reduction

Finding Balance: Enjoyment vs. Financial Goals

Finding balance between enjoyment and financial goals is a crucial aspect of achieving overall well-being, especially for individuals and families living on low to medium incomes. In a world where financial responsibilities often weigh heavily on our shoulders, it's essential to create a lifestyle that allows for both enjoyment and prudent money management. Striking this balance can lead to a more fulfilling life, where you can savor experiences and still work towards your financial aspirations.

The first step in this journey is to understand that enjoyment does not have to come at the expense of your financial goals. In fact, when approached correctly, they can complement each other beautifully. By identifying what truly brings you joy, you can allocate resources more effectively. Whether it's dining out occasionally, pursuing hobbies, or spending quality time with loved ones, these moments of enjoyment can motivate you to stay disciplined with your financial planning. Think of it this way: each dollar spent on something that brings genuine happiness is an investment in your well-being.

Next, consider the power of automating your finances. By setting up automatic transfers to savings accounts, debt repayments, and investment funds, you can create a system that works for you without constant oversight. This automation frees up mental space, allowing you to enjoy life more fully, while ensuring that your financial goals are met. High-interest savings accounts with no fees can serve as an excellent tool for growing your emergency fund and enabling you to enjoy life's little pleasures without the nagging worry about your financial health.

For those looking to manage major expenses, such as buying a car or planning a wedding, it's important to approach these milestones with a clear budget that allows for enjoyment. Establishing a realistic spending plan helps to alleviate the stress often associated with significant financial commitments. This can be achieved by prioritizing your spending, identifying areas where you can cut costs, and finding ways to celebrate these life events without overspending. Employing negotiation tactics for salary increases or using scripts to avoid late fees can also contribute to a more balanced financial life.

Ultimately, finding balance is about making conscious choices that align with your values and long-term goals. By embracing lifestyle adjustments that prioritize debt reduction while still allowing for enjoyment, you can create a sustainable financial path. Remember, your financial journey is not just about eliminating debt or increasing savings; it's about crafting a life where financial health and personal happiness coexist. Embrace the process, celebrate your victories, and understand that achieving balance is a journey worth taking.

Smart Spending Habits

Smart spending habits are the cornerstone of financial stability, particularly for individuals and families navigating the challenges of low and medium incomes. In a world where every dollar counts, cultivating a mindset focused on intentionality and purpose can transform your financial landscape. By embracing smart spending, you not only empower yourself to eliminate debt and save for the future but also create a life that aligns with your values and aspirations. This journey begins with a commitment to understanding your financial habits and making conscious choices that reflect your priorities.

One of the most effective strategies for smart spending is to track your expenses meticulously. This practice allows you to gain insights into where your money goes and identify areas where you can cut back without sacrificing the joy in your life. Consider using budgeting apps or simple spreadsheets to categorize your spending. By analyzing your habits, you can spot trends—such as frequent dining out or impulse purchases—that may be draining your resources. This awareness lays the groundwork for making informed decisions that will help you redirect funds toward debt repayment or savings. Embrace the power of knowledge, and watch as your financial situation begins to shift in your favor.

In addition to tracking expenses, opening no-fee, high-interest bank accounts is a smart spending habit that can yield significant benefits. Many individuals overlook the potential of their savings accounts, allowing traditional banks to erode their earnings through fees and low interest rates. Research online banks or credit unions that offer accounts with competitive interest rates and no hidden charges. By making this simple switch, you can keep your savings intact while earning more on your hard-earned dollars. This strategy not only enhances your savings but also reinforces your commitment to making your money work for you—an essential principle in building wealth.

Automating your finances is another key component of smart spending habits. By setting up automatic transfers to savings and debt repayment accounts, you create a system that prioritizes your financial goals without requiring constant attention. This strategy minimizes the temptation to spend money that should be allocated elsewhere. Tools like direct deposit and auto-billing can streamline your financial processes, ensuring that your money goes exactly where you want it. When you implement automation, you can focus on enjoying life while knowing that your financial health is steadily improving.

Finally, mastering the art of negotiation can significantly enhance your smart spending practices. Whether you're discussing a raise with your employer or negotiating lower rates on bills and subscriptions, effective communication can yield substantial savings. Prepare scripts that articulate your value or your situation clearly and confidently. By being proactive about your finances and not shying away from discussions that could lead to better terms, you position yourself as an empowered participant in your financial journey. These small changes in mindset and approach can lead to monumental shifts in your financial well-being, allowing you to spend wisely while still enjoying the richness of life.

Creating a Debt-Free Lifestyle

Creating a debt-free lifestyle is more than just a financial goal; it is a transformative journey that empowers you to regain control over your finances and your life. For many individuals living on low to medium incomes, the burden of debt can feel overwhelming. However, by adopting effective strategies and a positive mindset, you can eliminate debt faster than you ever imagined. This chapter will guide you through practical steps to cultivate a debt-free lifestyle, enabling you to enjoy the freedom that comes with financial independence.

To begin your journey, it's essential to understand the various debt repayment strategies available. Whether you're navigating student loans or credit card debt, techniques such as the snowball or avalanche method can be game-changers. The snowball method encourages you to pay off smaller debts first, providing quick wins that boost your motivation. On the other hand, the avalanche method focuses on tackling high-interest debts first, ultimately saving you money in the long run. By selecting a strategy that resonates with you, you can create a personalized debt repayment plan that aligns with your lifestyle, ensuring that each payment brings you closer to financial freedom.

As you embark on this path, consider making the most of high-interest savings accounts that don't drain your resources with excessive fees. These accounts allow your savings to grow without the burden of hidden costs, serving as a crucial tool in your financial toolkit. By automating your savings, you can effortlessly set aside funds for debt repayment and emergencies alike. Automating your finances, ensures that your money is directed to the right places without requiring constant vigilance. This hands-off approach not only simplifies your financial management but also empowers you to focus on achieving your goals.

Effective communication is another powerful tool in your debt-free journey. Late fees can derail your progress, but with prepared scripts for negotiating with creditors, you can avoid these pitfalls. Clearly explaining your situation and expressing your commitment to repayment can often yield favorable outcomes. Additionally, consider budgeting techniques that allow for enjoyment while maintaining financial discipline. By embracing a lifestyle that balances saving and spending, you can still indulge in the things you love without compromising your financial future.

Finally, as you work towards a debt-free lifestyle, keep in mind that significant life events, such as buying a car or planning a wedding, don't have to be financially stressful. With careful planning and strategic financial management, you can navigate these milestones with ease. Incorporating passive investment strategies will also enhance your wealth-building potential, allowing you to grow your resources without the complexity that often accompanies traditional investment methods. Remember, creating a debt-free lifestyle is a continuous journey filled with opportunities for growth, resilience, and empowerment. Embrace it wholeheartedly, and the rewards will be profound.

Conclusion: Your Roadmap to

Financial Freedom

Recap of Key Strategies

In the journey toward financial freedom, the key strategies outlined in "Automate Your Wealth" serve as essential tools for individuals with low and medium incomes. This recap aims to crystallize these strategies, empowering readers to take control of their financial destiny. Each approach is designed not only to streamline finances but also to instill a sense of confidence and capability. By focusing on actionable steps, anyone can eliminate debt, build savings, and invest wisely, all while maintaining the joys of everyday life.

One of the most powerful strategies discussed is the approach to eliminating debt and student loans more swiftly than one might believe possible. By implementing methods such as the snowball or avalanche debt repayment strategies, individuals can prioritize their payments effectively. This not only accelerates the journey to being debt-free but also fosters a sense of accomplishment with each milestone reached. For recent graduates, specific tips and techniques reveal how to tackle student loans head-on, transforming what often feels like an insurmountable burden into manageable steps toward financial liberation.

Equally important is the guidance on opening no-fee, high-interest bank accounts. This strategy ensures that hard-earned money works for you rather than draining your savings through hidden fees. By taking the time to research and select the right financial institutions, readers can maximize their savings potential. The book emphasizes the significance of automating finances. This approach allows individuals to set up automatic transfers to savings and investment accounts, ensuring that money flows exactly where it is needed without the constant need for manual intervention.

Avoiding late fees is another crucial element of financial health, and the book provides effective scripts to communicate with creditors. These step-by-step guides not only help individuals manage their bills more effectively but also cultivate a proactive approach to personal finance. Techniques for budgeting that prioritize enjoyment are also explored, allowing readers to save hundreds or even thousands each month without sacrificing the pleasures of life. By integrating these budgeting techniques into daily routines, one can achieve a balance that fosters both financial responsibility and personal satisfaction.

Lastly, the strategies for managing major life expenses are invaluable. Whether planning for a wedding, buying a car, or preparing for the arrival of a child, knowing how to navigate these financial milestones is critical. The book also delves into passive investment strategies, simplifying the process of wealth building for beginners. With precise language for negotiating a raise at work, readers can advocate for themselves effectively, leading to increased earnings that can further enhance their financial stability. By following these key strategies, the path to financial empowerment becomes not just a dream but a tangible reality within reach.

Creating Your Personalized Financial Plan

Creating a personalized financial plan is not just a necessity; it's a powerful tool that can transform your financial future. For those with low and medium incomes, the idea of managing finances might feel overwhelming. However, by taking charge of your financial landscape, you can carve out a path to financial stability and freedom. This journey begins with understanding your unique financial situation and setting clear, achievable goals. Whether you aim to eliminate debt, save for a major purchase, or build an emergency fund, your personalized financial plan will serve as a compass to guide you.

Start by assessing your current financial state. Gather all your financial statements, including income, expenses, debts, and savings. This comprehensive overview will help you identify where your money is going and where you can make adjustments. Next, outline your short-term and long-term financial goals. Short-term goals may include paying off credit cards or building an emergency fund, while long-term goals might involve saving for a home or retirement. By breaking down these goals into manageable steps, you create actionable plans that can lead to meaningful progress.

Automating your finances is a game changer, particularly for busy professionals. Utilizing tools that allow you to set up automatic transfers to savings accounts or debt repayments can streamline your financial management. For instance, consider opening a no-fee, high-interest savings account that allows your money to grow without unnecessary costs. Automating these processes removes the burden of remembering deadlines and helps you avoid late fees, ultimately ensuring that your money goes exactly where you want it. Embrace the simplicity of automation and watch as your financial worries begin to dissipate.

Effective budgeting is essential for enjoying life while still working toward your financial goals. This doesn't mean sacrificing the things you love; rather, it involves making informed choices about where to allocate your resources. Use budgeting techniques that allow for flexibility and fun, ensuring you can enjoy life's pleasures without derailing your financial plan. By implementing lifestyle adjustments that prioritize both enjoyment and debt reduction, you can find a balance that fosters financial wellness and satisfaction.

Finally, remember that your financial plan is a living document. Life is unpredictable, and your circumstances will evolve over time. Regularly review and adjust your plan to reflect changes in income, expenses, and life events. Whether you're negotiating a raise at work, preparing for a new family member, or planning a major purchase, the ability to adapt your financial strategy will keep you on track. With a personalized financial plan in place, you empower yourself to navigate challenges and celebrate successes, all while building a brighter financial future.

Staying Motivated on Your Journey to Build Wealth

Staying motivated on your wealth journey is essential, especially for those of us navigating the complexities of debt, savings, and investment with limited incomes. It's easy to feel overwhelmed by financial goals that seem distant or unattainable. However, by breaking down your journey into manageable steps and celebrating small victories along the way, you can maintain a positive mindset and keep your momentum going. Remember, every little progress counts, and the path to financial stability is not a sprint but a marathon.

One effective way to boost your motivation is to visualize your goals clearly. Whether you're aiming to eliminate student loans, save for a dream vacation, or build an emergency fund, creating a vivid picture of what success looks like can inspire you on tough days. Consider maintaining a vision board or setting up reminders of your financial milestones on your phone. This constant visual cue can serve as a powerful motivator, pushing you to stick to your budget, automate your finances, and keep your spending in check.

Additionally, surround yourself with positivity and support. Engage with communities that share similar financial goals, whether online or in-person. Sharing your experiences with others on the same journey can provide encouragement, accountability, and valuable insights. Celebrate each other's successes, no matter how small, and use those moments as motivation to keep pushing forward. Remember, your wealth journey is unique, and it's crucial to find inspiration in the progress of others without comparing your path to theirs.

Implementing practical strategies can also keep your motivation high. Automating your finances, for instance, allows you to take the guesswork out of saving and investing. By setting up automatic transfers to high-interest savings accounts or investment platforms, you can watch your wealth grow without constant effort. This hands-off approach not only simplifies the process but also reinforces the idea that your financial goals are within reach. Knowing that your money is actively working for you can offer a significant boost to your motivation.

Finally, embrace a mindset of gratitude and accomplishment. Recognize and appreciate how far you've come, even if it feels small. Each payment made towards debt or each month of savings is a step towards a more secure financial future. Acknowledge your efforts and understand that financial growth does not happen overnight. Celebrate your journey, commit to your financial goals, and remember that staying motivated is about finding joy in the process as much as the end result. With each step you take, you're building not just wealth, but a more confident and empowered version of yourself.

www.ingramcontent.com/pod-product-compliance
Lightning Source LLC
Chambersburg PA
CBHW070415230526
45471CB00006B/2810